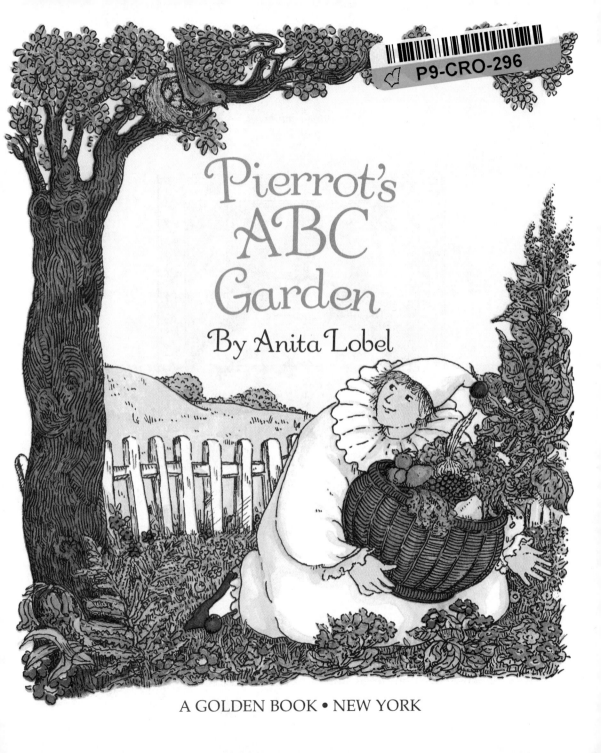

Pierrot's ABC Garden

By Anita Lobel

A GOLDEN BOOK • NEW YORK

for little Lena Lobel,
with love

Published on the occasion of
the 50th anniversary of Little Golden Books

Western Publishing Company, Inc., Racine, Wisconsin 53404

Pierrot missed his friend Pierrette.

One morning Pierrot said to his pigs
and sheep,
"I will go and visit Pierrette.

"And I will bring her something
from my garden."

He went and found some **Asparagus**

and **Beets**

and **Celery**

and **Dandelion** greens.

Then he picked an **Eggplant**

and **Flowers**

and **Grapes**

and **Hazelnuts**.

He gathered **Indian figs**

and **Juniper berries**

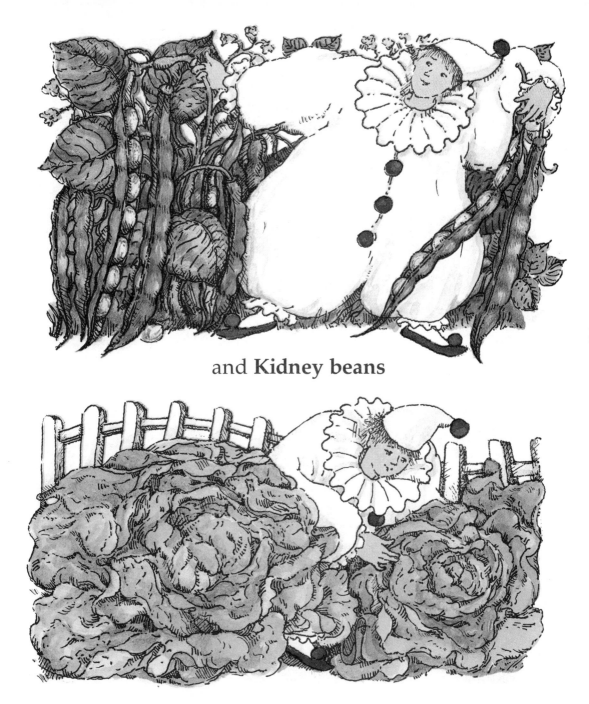

and **Kidney beans**

and **Lettuce**.

He also found **Mushrooms**

and **Nectarines**

and **Onions**

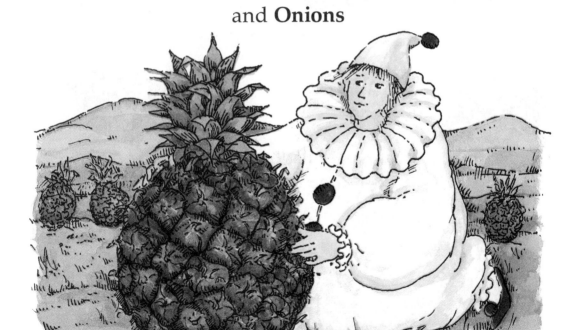

and even a **Pineapple**.

He picked **Quince**

and **Rhubarb**

and **Strawberries**

and **Tomatoes**.

Under a tree he
found an abandoned
Ukelele and a **Vase**

and a **Whirligig**
and a **Xylophone**.

"These are good presents, too," thought Pierrot.

Pierrot's basket was very full.

"Now **You** can help me," Pierrot
said to a **Zebra** standing alone.

"Good-bye, good-bye," Pierrot said to the sheep and the pigs.

Then he and the zebra carrying the basket walked all the way to Pierrette's house.

"What good things you have brought!"
cried Pierrette, running to kiss her friend
Pierrot. She was very happy to see him.

They had a fine picnic. They ate the good
things from Pierrot's garden. They played
and sang. Pierrot's pigs and sheep came, too.

At the end of the day, they went to
sleep and dreamed very happy dreams.